Invasive Species

poems by

Michelle Lizet Flores

Finishing Line Press
Georgetown, Kentucky

Invasive Species

Copyright © 2024 by Michelle Lizet Flores
ISBN 979-8-88838-456-5 First Edition
All rights reserved under International and Pan-American Copyright Conventions. No part of this book may be reproduced in any manner whatsoever without written permission from the publisher, except in the case of brief quotations embodied in critical articles and reviews.

ACKNOWLEDGMENTS

I'd like to thank the following publications where versions of these poems first appeared or will appear:

- *Badlands:* "Guajira Trapped in the States" (2011)
- *The Miami Rail:* "Florida Gothic #2: Hogar" and "Florida Gothic #3: I-10 to Lake City" (2017)
- *Noble/Gas Quarterly:* "Giving Up La Lucha" (2017)
- *Gravel Magazine:* "Self-Taught Motherhood" (2018)
- *Azahores:* "Eliseo," "Sugarloaf Key," and "My abuela was a seamstress" (2018)
- *Rigorous:* "Mateo Sings the Blues", "Of Dora and Diego", "Florida Gothic #4: No Sleep 'til JAX", "My [   ] was a Racist" (2018)
- *Cagibi:* "Hurricane Season" (2018)
- *Clockhouse:* "The Flying Flor" (2018)
- *Cosmonauts Avenue:* "Movement" (2018)
- *The Ear:* "God moves in mysterious ways." (2018)
- *The Acentos Review:* "A Series of Facebook Updates after Hurricane Irma" (2018)
- *Bridge Eight Online:* "Conjuro for the Lonely Daugther" (2019)
- *Chiricú Journal:* "15 Ways of Looking at a Latina" (2019)

The following poems were originally published in the chapbook *Cuentos from the Swamp* (2019)
- "Hurricane Day"
- "Alone"
- "Dressing my Mother"

The following poems were originally published in the chapbook *Memoria* (2020)
- "Naranja y Sal"
- "Heirloom"

Publisher: Leah Huete de Maines
Editor: Christen Kincaid
Cover Art: Dimelza Broche painting *The Upside Down*
Author Photo: Jose Luis Alonso Jr.
Cover Design: Elizabeth Maines McCleavy

Order online: www.finishinglinepress.com
also available on amazon.com

Author inquiries and mail orders:
Finishing Line Press
PO Box 1626
Georgetown, Kentucky 40324
USA

Table of Contents

Ritual 1

Before

Arcelia Vega del Toro 5

My abuela was a seamstress 6

Guajira Trapped in the States 7

The Flying Flor 8

Florida Gothic #5: Invasive Species 9

Sugarloaf Key 11

Florida Gothic #6: Tent Revival in Overtown 12

October 2004 14

Florida Gothic #2: Hogar 15

During

Hurricane Season 19

Movement 20

Alone 21

Dressing my Mother 22

Carve and Release 23

God moves in mysterious ways. 25

Reversal 27

Nostalgia 28

People keep telling me how alike we look. 29

Giving Up La Lucha 30

After

Hurricane Day 33

The Way Things Should Have Gone 34

After Fornicating with a Stranger 35

My last real conversation with Mami. 36

Eliseo 37

Affirmations 39

Florida Gothic #4: No Sleep 'til JAX 40

I want to be 41

Bautizada 42

Rebirth

Florida Gothic #7: After the Hurricane 47

Dar la Luz 49

Self-Taught Motherhood 52

Mateo Sings the Blues 53

Desarraigada 54

Conjuro for the Lonely Daughter 55

Florida Gothic #3: I-10 to Lake City 57

Just smile more. 58

A series of Facebook updates after Hurricane Irma. 59

Naranja y Sal. 61

15 Ways of Looking at a Latina 63

My [   ] was a racist. 64

I'm not white but… 67

Heirloom 69

When you turn 52. 71

Acknowledgments

For Lizet P. Flores

Ritual

Begin by boiling water.
Pour a tablespoon of honey into your mug
let a tea bag soak it up.
wait until the kettle whistles
empty its contents for your drink.

    [read: *elixir*]

Pull a plate out of the cupboard.
Fill it with freshly rinsed grapes
and cubes of pepper jack cheese.

    [read: *offerings*]

Find your best water glass
the one you bought at the vintage shop
the one you can't put in the dishwasher.
Fill it with crisp, cool water.

Set your table.

    [read: *altar*]

The alimentos to your left.
The poems to your right.
Your computer in the center.

    [read: *trinity*]

And this is where your mother will speak to you

    unlocking the words you keep trapped in your chest.

And this is where your grandfather will play his guitar

    helping you find the rhythm to each line.

And this is where your bisabuela will guide you

teaching you how to heal with words rather than herbs.

Alchemy creates more than gold if you give it time.

I.
Before

Arcelia Vega del Toro

Born in El Oriente, she was the descendant of a long line of Cuban Mambises—revolutionaries who sought independence from Spain. A guajira through and through, she learned under the full moon and near waterfalls: how to help women give their light, how her voice could be used to call on the Orishas, which herbs healed and soothed each part of a body, why blood was the only gift that really got things done. People came from all over Cuba, carrying chickens and goats over mountains to reach her. One day, the town doctor died. It mourned their only learned man's passing. For all her knowledge of life, Arcelia would never fully stop death. That night, santeros beat their drums, spices and smoke filling the air as she stared dry-eyed into the clouds covering the moon. While at the burial, she turned from the crowd, walking towards the rotting tombstones in the deepest recesses of the cemetery. Slowly, she lifted the stones out of their resting places, piling each one on the other. When she built her mountain, she climbed to the top and fell asleep. Santeros, in their white linen garb, surrounded her. Their tiny red beads swayed against their chests as they prayed to Oya, keeper of the cemetery, giving her eggplant, goat, and black horsehair. At midnight, Arcelia awoke, leaving the santeros to their worship. She walked back to her finca and gazed at the waterfall where her ten daughters played. She prayed to Oshun, protector of the rivers. As her daughters fell asleep beneath the stars, she stepped towards the cascade and filled her hands with water. She walked to the house, to her husband and three sons, hands cupped so tightly the water could not escape. Death would not touch them that night.

My abuela was a seamstress.

In memory of the Triangle Shirtwaist Factory Fire of 1911

She sewed many things:
        bathing suits, dresses, jackets, buttons.

She too found place in the New York sweatshops
        trading fabrica for factoria,
        lavandería for laundri,
        El Oriente for Brooklyn.

These women.
Their work.

The chains on each door—
the thread in each bobbin—
the prick of each needle—

Did their nietas wonder
why they didn't make it home
for dinner that night?

Were their lovers waiting
beneath a marquee?

These women
flinging themselves
out of windows,

their blood runs

        in the air

           in me.

Guajira Trapped in the States

She leaves El Oriente because Mami says
life will be better this way. So at seventeen,
in a new country farther north than she's
ever imagined, she sews. She can make
everything she could never afford to buy.

Hazel eyes are quickly masked by purple moons.
Hands that once swam through lakes now hem skirts.
Lips that once kissed guayabas now grip hat pins.
Feet that once climbed mountains now tap a pedal.

Years go by. While Brooklyn stiffens
her joints, Miami calls.

As the seasons give way to the land
where the trees don't sleep, her hands
remember what her mind forgot: Guajira,
with some eggshells and carrot shavings,
makes the mangoes healthy once more.
Where she steps, orchids rise, growing
because she gave them breath.

Yet still, Miami is not home.

Guajira reads her Biblia outside as the sun
goes down. She drifts to sleep and dreams
of her Cuba,
        y su finca,
                y su cascada.

The Flying Flor

She floats, suspended around the waste from our rusty swing set by the neon green jump rope I won after selling eight boxes of the world's finest chocolate, her deep brown hair flying around her freckled face, her lips hugging her oversized teeth while she sings her Spanish songs, arms raised, calling on the winds to pick her up and take her away; for a moment they do, but I lose faith and there she falls, the glitter-filled rope snapping, releasing her down to the ground in a daze of terrified giggles and flailing limbs.

As I run to her, she rolls over, face contorted, a fallen seraph punctured by the blades of grass, while Abuela scuttles outside, ammonia and brown dye number 37 dripping down her cheek, melting her brows into hazel eyes, hands still covered by too-big plastic gloves; she picks up The Flying Flor, smacks her, checks to see if she's all right, then comes after me, popping my nalgas before I have time to brace myself.

I limp towards my broken jump rope as she is carried inside, the neon stretched to whiteness, dreams of greatness dashed as I realize hubris is the lie we tell ourselves when we attempt to fly without wings.

Florida Gothic #5: Invasive Species

One.
You hear the croaking when you wake in the middle of the night.
A chorus of cane toads singing to the moon.
You rise and slip from bedroom to hallway to kitchen
for a cold glass of water
using the red goblets Mami bought on sale at Ross.

You look at your reflection
in the black window
a silhouette of flowing cotton and greasy hair.

You leave the empty glass by the sink,
    watch as the grass quivers in crescent moon light,
        as the palm fronds drip with humidity.

You slip back to your bed,
the hairs on the back of your neck alert.
They follow the eyes that keep watching.
You stiffly drift back to sleep.

Two.
You are 5 or 7 years old.
Your father stands with a carton of iodized salt
(the kind in that deep blue container with the little girl in the yellow rain jacket).

It's just finished raining and the Miami dusk shrouds the world in a sage filter.
He opens the spout and pours the salt in his hand—
    waiting.

The cane toad creeps out of the hedge and onto the sidewalk.
Your father throws the salt in a flash,
the toad now a rusty red.

Belly up, its legs scratch at the air like a cockroach's.

Papi upends the container and pours enough to make the creature melt.

You sneak forward, pincers ready to grasp it.

He pulls your arm back and walks you inside.

Sugarloaf Key

For the first time in a long time,
I can see the stars.
Hell, I can see the Milky Way—
the sky is finally more than a haze of street lamps.
Papi's putting away the fishing poles while
Mom and Nicky play a card game of ten phases.
I can never remember the rules.

I hear the ocean. It drifts in and out.
I want to dive in the dark water.
I want to search for jellyfish and mermaids.
I want to find Atlantis and see what all the fuss is about.

"Chelly," Papi calls. "Ven aquí. Hold me this."
He passes me a plate of steaks for the grill.
Sirens beckon me towards the water, but we have to eat.
Our tent shakes in a gust of wind.

"Dame el plato." He takes the plate from my hands
and I set the table. The sirens give up, moving further
south, perhaps to Key West or to Cuba.

"Gorda?" Mom calls me out of my thoughts. "Let's eat."
She hangs the lantern over the picnic table.
The sky is just a grey haze again.

Florida Gothic #6: Tent Revival in Overtown.

Three in the afternoon. Sweltering Miami heat. August.

We've come to save souls with our Word and Worship and Glory.

Pastor Jeff carries the gallon of olive oil. He says a prayer and holds it to the sun. Then he comes to each of us, dripping ribbons on our open palms as we break off into the sides of the green space.

Later, we gather poles and canvas and we spread around this newly hallowed ground and Brother Pino, with his mallet, beats the stakes into earth.

We string the lights across the edge of the canvas.
We hoist the horizontal pole to hold the tent up

    and here is where we will find God.

As the sun dims across the downtown skyline,
men and women from the neighborhood come
to join us in the newly hallowed space
our black and brown and pale faces glowing in the dusk.

The offering plate is passed—
    we find dollars and needles and coins and menthols
        and we find the Spirit
        and we find the things that make us ugly but make us numb.

And somewhere between the twilight and the glowing orange mist I find a space where I'm supposed to believe

    yet I can't feel anything.

And I find a space where I've learned to speak in tongues
      where I've learned to slay myself in the spirit

    yet I still feel nothing.

I convince myself
      that my faith is in my actions
      not my words.

As these men and women slowly sweep away back to their homes
                              to their streets,
we the teens in this rescue mission
we gather and I watch as we talk and laugh
and I think of Thomas.

You see he doubted
but this numbness
is not that.

I found nothing in this
portable temple.

Call me Lilith
Call me Ruth
Call me Bitch
Call me Truth

I am legion. I feel none.

October 2004

So it's
Abuela's kitchen in the fall and
Bananas with my rice and beans and sopa de
Calabasa on the stove and abuela yelling
"Donde poniste el tenedor Michelle?" and
Every time I think of her I
Feel like aguacate on the back of a spoon like
Greasy hair after a morning of limpiando la casa.
Horas pass as we bread croquetas and
I wonder if she learned this from her grandmother
Just as I'm learning this from her
Keeping these recetas in my fingers
Licking the salt and fat and bread
My tongue a book a blade
Now a peacock
"¡Oiga!" She yells. "Eso hace daño."
"¿Porque me gritas abuela?" I ask,
Questioning this woman who climbed water falls and survived sweatshops and
Remembers what it feels like to be the new girl in the land of Anglos and their bullshit.
"Señorita, te faltas el respeto."
That tone of hers, the way she cuts with breath
Under my ribs where the meat is still sweet and I know I'm a
Virgin but she still tells me my hips are getting bigger
Whatever that means.
Xiomara calls her personal line and she hides herself in her room.
"Ya terminaste abuela?" I call.
Zephyrs caress the mango tree, flowing through the open windows as the sun finally sets.

Florida Gothic #2: Hogar

A squirrel nibbles at
       a fallen mamey.

Abuela ties a plastic lizard to
       the mango tree. A white cat strolls along
       the fence, eyeing her.

Abuela doesn't notice and continues to

       hum her ballads.

Feral peacocks call from

       the distance.

I float on
       a vinyl purple flower.
My thighs stick to
       the surface though
I try to
       moisten them with
       gentle splashes of chlorinated salvation.

My outer arms warm to
       a golden brown color, like melted butter in
       a copper skillet.

My inner arms embrace their cool pale tone,
       blue veins peeking through

fish in
a frozen river.

The banyan trees begin to
grow where they had been cut last hurricane season,
       short green branches bursting from
flat brown knots.

I hop out of

the pool to
stare at the bougainvillea. I lay my towel beneath
and peer at
a fuchsia filtered sky.

A cane toad rests by
my ankles.

Mosquitoes and gnats buzz past, finding rotten guava a few feet from me.
The scent makes my head
       spin and soon I lose track of
time and space.

Suddenly
or
a few hours later
the sky is a midnight blue.

More cane toads arrive,
       calling out
              to the moon.

II.
During

Hurricane Season

The sky is an orange haze. Miami
is cooler than she has been this
summer. Rain drips into the pool.
It is now filled with one thousand
rings crashing through one another.
A snake scrapes against the bottom,
sucking up scum and seeds.
Palm fronds wave in the warm,
wet wind, and suddenly, Kendall
Village's last will-o'-wisp floats
towards me. She falls on my knee
and quietly sputters out. Whether
she sleeps or dies, I do not know.
I merely pick her up and lay her
by my side. Together, we watch
as our world slowly melts away.

Movement

It started with the ovaries.
    The doctor plucked one out
    before you ever bedded anyone.
Next came the spine.
    The scar nearly fades into your dusting of freckles,
though in certain
    lights its raised skin glints: spilled oil.
The thyroid was the first to be deadly.
    I was eight years old trying to see a world
    without your singing.
Your left breast followed.
    I was in calculus learning tangents when I noticed, on the glossy
    surface of my desk, how we have the same mouth.
Now it's your brain.
    That fucking golf ball—

Alone

Her head is in my hands
now. Hair shaven, eyes
closed. A yin and yang
of skin and scar. Gently,
I rub her velvet scalp,
careful to avoid the fading
sutures. She smiles, eyes
still closed as she drifts
off to sleep.

Curious, I slowly brush my left
finger across the C-shaped scar.
Hair and thread poke my finger
tip, and a sharp intake of breath
tells me she's awake.

"Careful," she says.

"Sorry, Mom."

"Don't leave me."

"I'm not going anywhere."

Her breathing slows. I lean in
to kiss her cheek. She quickly
pulls the sheet over her face.
The shadows from the bedside
lamp create a forest in which
I find myself lost.

Dressing my Mother

She tries to sit on the toilet but falls,
nearly knocking her head against the bidet.

My sister and I hold her up
while our cousin dries her off.

We slip on her panties, then bra,
smoothing lotion on her skin.

It seems freckles spread since last time I looked.

I clip the bra over the scar on her spine.
I hold her up as she lifts one leg, then the other.

Her eyes are covered by purple moons.

We slip the black shirt over her arms.
We walk to bed and as she plops down, she cries.

I smooth her hair with Agua de Violetas.
She spikes it back up.

I hold her hand as Nicky tells her everyone falls.
When she stops crying, I go to my room.

I won't let her watch me break.

Carve and Release

After the doctors cut the tumors out of my mother,
after the year and a half of chemo and radiation,
after her jaw began to sag and her eyelids drooped,

    my mother began to remember.

It was during her first year in Miami.
Lizet was new to the city,
    to her teenage body,
when her grandfather spied on her through the crack in the door.
She was hanging the one red blouse she wore every Friday.

Maybe she was too beautiful,
    with her thin arms
    and black hair that grazed
    the tops of her guitarlike hips.

Maybe he just couldn't believe that someone so beautiful could be a part of him.

Whatever the reason,
he glided into the room,
grasped her from behind,
and touched the breasts
she was still growing into,
the legs that never
seemed to end,
all the while describing
the ways he could love her.

She was still holding the red blouse, crumpling the lace in her hands
unable to move.

There was no prince to help her,
    no knighted brothers
        or angelic savior.

But she did have a guajira mother who stormed
into the room after a day of roaming Hialeah.

Olga crushed his guitarrista hands as she thrust
him into the burning Miami sun. She held her daughter's
face and muttered a prayer Lizet could not understand.
She led her to the shower—
told her to clean herself,
to never speak of the incident again.

Mami didn't cry as she remembered this.
We lay in bed together.

I let my breathing match hers.
She asked me to rub her scalp.
I grazed the tufts of baby hair
that grew over the C-shaped scar.

God moves in mysterious ways.

I knelt for my mother
at the altar.
I was not greedy,
never asked
for a miracle.
I just wanted God
to give her strength
and rest.

Four days later
she had a stroke.

I used to tell myself
evil was not God's fault—
bad things happen.
All we can do is move on.
Knowing this does not
make it hurt
any less.

Now I wonder if I
have ever believed.
There is a hole
in my chest
no Spirit
could fill.

My mother has been dying
for a year and a half now.
She's lost in
her own eyes.
She hears bells
I wish I could—
a ringing that keeps
her awake
praying.

All I can hear her repeat
is *Oh, Lord, my Father.*

I can't help but wonder
if He's purposefully
ignoring her.

Children should bury
their parents. That is the order
of things.
Knowing this does not
make the digging
any easier.

Reversal

For a few weeks, my skin was tight.
I could barely lift my arms above
my head.

Abuela said to rub the gooey aloe
against my copper skin, but I couldn't
bring myself to cut the leaves off the rosette.
So instead, I soaked in the pain.

For a while there, the acne scars that line
my face were a dull memory beneath
my cheeks colorado.

This was the first time my sister's
café con leche skin paled against
the glow of my cinnamon flesh.

Now she was the one awake at all hours
of the night, patrolling the cardiac unit
in her Mickey Mouse scrubs while I spent
my days poolside armed with heart-shaped
sunglasses and an airport novel.

She was doing things the right way
growing up, preparing for motherhood,
as Mami slowly died.

I indulged in what I missed out—
coming home just before dawn,
drinking 'til strangers became beautiful.

But as the summer came to a close,
my skin began falling off,
freeing the pale olive tones.

Beach days and bike rides.
Spilled whiskey became
dust at my feet.

Nostalgia

I wish I could keep you forever.
I have your blood,
      your skin,
        your all too serious face.
Soon it will be me, alone
in a forest of phosphorescent trees.
I'll search for you in the stars, in the earth.
I'd change myself into a hawk for you. I'd stay that way
forever—the first of my kind,
then darkness would not be strange in my eyes.

People keep telling me how alike we look.

I can still smell your soap,
detergent, and musky perfume.

Maybe if I rub my head on your pillow,
I'll find one of your hairs.

Maybe if I close my eyes,
God will speak to me.

If had known you'd be gone in five years…
Maybe that's why we fought so much.

You wanted to keep me then,
as I want to keep you now.

I keep biting my lips—perhaps their shape will change.

I find myself in your closet
pulling on your dresses.

Giving Up La Lucha

This dress of yours, the A-line way it hangs off my body,
the bosom that's a bit too big,
it's the last thing I'll wear in front of you.

Nicky tells me I look like a diva,
with straight hair and heart-shaped
sunglasses hiding my face.

Five months ago sabía.
Five months ago.

I couldn't touch the coffin 'til now,
as it waited for the stygian to lower it into the cement box
to protect it from earth.

I left two flowers and a kiss for you.
I didn't speak. The choir didn't want to hear what I had to say.
They think you're in heaven now.

Then came that concrete slab sealing you in
a world of rotting roses and pine.

Your brother shoveled dirt into your grave. I could see it
wander in the wind. I could feel the sun burn
as the viejos did the same.

Then the dump truck came.

My soul reached out for that shovel.

My feet stayed planted on the earth

III.
After

Hurricane Day

I dive into the cold briny water. October winds roll the waves towards shore. I kick my way to the ocean while I stare at the waves above me, the cloudy jade water breaking, forcing me down onto the sand. I pop up for air, and a wave smashes into my face. I laugh and cough, diving back before another can hit me. I look eerie beneath the surface. My skin hasn't seen real sunlight in almost five months. I am ghost, a victim of the siren's call, trying to make my way back to my ship. As I glide back up, I scan the shore. My sister sits with her knees to her chest, arms wrapped around legs, and I slowly swim to her.

When the water is shallow enough, I climb onto the rough sand, plopping myself down beside her. She hides her face in her knees. Her long, black hair covers her back and shoulders. She peeks at me, head still pressed against her knees, eyes dry and dark. I pull some of the thick black curls away from her face.

"I miss her," she says. I glance at the water.

"I miss her too." We sit on the beach while tourists and teenagers shift about, playing soccer and blasting their radios. I wipe my eyes and lie on my back, squinting while staring at the bright sky above. Faint wisps of white float above me, then her hair whips against the sky. I prop myself up as she dives into the ocean. When she comes up for air, her hair floats around her. She turns towards shore, then slips back into the water. I sit up with my legs crossed, pushing my hands into the sand.

The Way Things Should Have Gone

I should have taken you by the hand,
walked you to my car,
opened the door for you,
helped you into your seat.
I should have driven the moment you suggested it,
riding on the Palmetto, away from the sunset,
towards the skyscrapers the cocaine cowboys built,
towards the beach you haven't been to since 1996,
when it was completely different than today's.
You should have complained about my driving
as I navigated my way through the hoards of chongas and tourists.
I should have parked in the 4th street lot. You would have
opened the door on your own, and together, we would walk
to the beach barefoot. We would have sat on the sand,
watching as the sky turned purple, then blue, then the darkest of grays,
but never black. That would have been the water's job.
And you would have smiled, pretending the lights dotting the horizon
weren't cruise ships.

I should have done all these things. But I didn't.
Instead I left. Because I wanted to.
Because you let me. Because I should have
taken you to the beach that Friday night, but my friends invited me
to a movie, the name of which I can't remember.

After Fornicating with a Stranger

She was born in Brooklyn,
just like this stranger.
I was too: second birth,
carnal salvation.

She lived above a candy
shop, sneaking penny
treats when my Abuelo
wasn't looking.

I live near a bar
where Jameson and Tecate
call my name each night.

He says *cawffee* and *watah* as she did,
though she spent thirty years
in suburbanized swampland.

Five years later I still can't
say *machete* in American.

Lying next to a snoring
body, I think of the decades
she spent lying next to my father.

I feel her through my windows,
lifting curtains, trying to expose me—
but I buried my faith with her.
His heart beats through
my fingertips.

The snoring stops and he wipes
my cheek, pulling me closer
and kissing my lips. I can't help
but wish I could tell her.

My last real conversation with Mami.

She told me she knew. She could feel her mind slipping, her voice cracking as the hymns in her synapses crumbled to dust. Mami looked at me as though she was trying to burn me into her pupils.

She said, "Your father's young."

She said, "He's a good man, better than me."

She said, "I didn't want him to defile my bed, but he is young. I've tried to love him one more time, but I can't, Gorda. I just can't. So if he meets someone, let him fall in love. He's a good man with needs."

She said through her tears, her spit.

I was still a virgin then—I didn't know what it meant to feel someone inside of myself, skin against skin.

If she were alive right now, she'd be ashamed of me—a girl who fucks a much older man to drive the pain away. The things I let him do to me… but what does it matter now?

I am a cane toad waiting in the night.

Eliseo

      Abuela Tata
          (clad in a bata de casa)
          (and chancletas)
opens the door and unlocks
the gate.

      Clay roof tiles,
          the width of an old man's thigh,
match the orange brick-like tiles leading to the front door.

      "¿Qué tal mi niñita?"

      "¿Qué tal Abuelita?"
      I kiss her on the cheek.
      Papi follows
          in the narrow hallway
towards the common area.

      Abuelo Eliseo sits
in his carved wooden rocking chair,
          the wicker backing fraying.

      He watches a baseball game on TV—
          sound off,
          with the radio tuned to the Spanish station.
He doesn't notice me 'til I kiss his cheek.

      "¿Qué estudias?" Abuelo asks.

      "La Poesía. Quiero ser Poeta."

His eyes turn from the TV.
His hand turns the volume down to a low murmur.

"Michelle," he began, "Cuando era joven,
        después de un partido de béisbol,
        iba al bar y cantaba Punto Guajiro.
        Parecía un desastre,
        sudado con mi uniforme todavía encendido,
        pero cantaba y la gente aplaudía.
        Leíamos Martí y bebíamos cerveza hasta
        que llegaba la hora de irme a casa."

Papi rolls his eyes, hiding a smile with his shrugging shoulders.

"¿En serio, Abuelito?" I ask.

He smiles,
        as though in pain.

"Chinita," he says. "No envejezcas."

Affirmations

One day I will wake up and I will not be tired.
One day someone will pay to read what I have to say.
One day I will be ready to be a mother.
One day I will be in the moment.
One day I will love myself.
One day I will stand and not wince.
One day I will look at my skin and see it glow.
One day I will smile without pain.
One day I will unclench my jaw.
One day my neck will relax.
One day I will wake up and be happy to be alive.

Florida Gothic #4: No Sleep 'til JAX

It's December
        but the trees won't sleep.

The grass is yellowing
        (dry season).

Beads of moisture
        collect on grimy
        plastic furniture.

It's midnight,
        yet
        I-95 is filled with cars northing to somewhere.

You change the radio station;
        the same song
        keeps playing,
        picking up where
        the last station left off.

You peer through the forests and hedges
        of the interstate
into backyards of
        empty patios
        lights twinkling and spinning—
        discos long forgotten.

Fog clings to the open road.
Orbs of light attempt to guide you
        home, but once you reach

the Everglades you are flung into deep space
        reflective bits of plastic acting like stars.
        Intergalactic caution signs
        drawing you to the void.

I want to be

A woman with a head full of grey hair—
happy and wrinkly—
a grandma.

I want to live in a shack
near the woods
in a house boat
on the swamp.

I want a life on my terms
full of art
and sunrises.

I want to dance
naked under the moon
and drink
until strangers glow.

I want to learn the
curanderismo
my bisabuela once practiced.

I want to cover
my body
in words—
talismans of manifestations.

I want to be everything
my mother
could never be.

I want to be whole.

Bautizada

It's midnight in September
and the ocean beckons me from the bar
I walk, alone with my friends
listen to her howl my name
yhink about the nights
I never finished
what I'd started.

We sit in the darkness,
catch glimpses of each other
as lightning flashes
just north of us.

In Boriken, there is a tradition
of falling into the ocean
backwards, blind
at the start of the new year.

Well, this year is only three-quarters through,
but time is an illusion
and I live to be immortal.

I stand, peel off my lace jacket,
then my black denim shorts.

I walk to the black waves before me
unsure of what creatures lie
beneath the surface
not caring—
for if I am to go, this would be the way,

but much like my ancestral sailors
who prayed to
Caridad del Cobre and Yemaya
I survive
beneath the waxing moon.

I am but a speck
      a memory

a reverie
        to the North Florida night.

IV.
Rebirth

Florida Gothic #7: After the Hurricane

It's a verifiable fact
that whiskey tastes best
when you drink it on your porch
while staring at an orange sky.

Hurricane winds bluster
through giant oak trees
and Spanish moss.

You wrap yourself in a tattered blanket—
the last gift your mother gave you
before she forgot your face.

Power lines bounce in the wind
the September air finally giving hints
of a season that never
quite takes hold.

You pull her fleece around your shoulders.
Cars brave enough to traverse
the flooded streets
veer slowly past
felled branches
and scattered pieces of home.

Half the state is under water.
The other half is out of power.

But you keep sipping your whiskey—
    keep smoking your menthols—
    keep staring duende in the face.

On nights like these, the humid air
finally gives way to the promise
of a future
where you can start again.

But then you remember
you live in Florida

where there are only two seasons:
before and after the storm.

Here, nothing lasts forever.

Dar la Luz

Surprise   Mistake
Desire   Numbing
Ignore   Avoid

Take your pill
Take your pill
Take your pill

Forget

Reveal the truth to yourself
                your sister
                him

Eat, drink, cry, read, walk, teach, grow
                                grow
                                grow

Feel the dance within—
    the touch near your ribs—
    the burning in your chest.

Grow
Grow
Grow

Don't ask yourself how to do it without her.
Don't ask yourself how she did it.
Don't ask yourself about her.

Just read. You expect too much.

Go through that maze
        of rooms
        of halls
        of elevators
        of beeping sounds

Find the bed
    the nurse(s)
    the doctor(s).

They fill you up.
You ask *with what*.
You try to understand.
You expect too much.

One day passes.
You can't leave the room.
You try to walk.
The nurses, the doctors—
they tie you back up to the bed.
They pop you open—
let you spill out of yourself.
You feel wet and painless.

Another day passes
You still feel nothing
But the pressure in your bowels.
The doctor says it's time to push.
The nurse says it's time to be calm.

You ask for water and they tell you no.
You ask for a cracker and they tell you no.
You ask for sleep and they tell you no.

You want to see your mother.
You want her hand on your shoulder
                your belly.
You want her to sing you a lullaby.

You expect too much.

You push and they pull and you keep pushing
but all you feel is a head trapped
between your legs.

You give up.
They expected too much.

They take you to the room
                  the altar.
They pull up the curtain
and you think of the Holy of Holies
        (even now, you aren't allowed)
and you feel them move your organs—
but you don't feel pain.

And slowly

but all at once

a baby

in his father's arms.

You see his face

and wonder

if you'd ever

really seen

a face before.

You begin to dream
while lucid
as they sew you
back together
and your mother
hums in your ear
before
you wake again.

Self-Taught Motherhood

Did she get lost in my soft brown eyes the way I get lost in hers?
        In the curl of my lashes
                The grip of my fists

Did she run her fingers through the thick black fluff on my scalp?
        Over my ever filling cheeks
                The spaces between my toes

Did she nurse me like I nurse her?
        On my side
                The blankets smelling of milk and Agua de Violetas

Did I fall asleep in her arms?
        With a full belly
               The sunlight making us glow

Did she make voices while she read to me?
        Near a window
               The wind and rain offsetting her joy

Did she sing a healing spell?
After I bumped my head on a dresser
              The words "Sana, sana, colita de rana…"

Did she know I'd somehow remember these moments?
        Through muscle memory
                The grief tasting like bitter coffee and raw sugar.

Mateo Sings the Blues

After Hurricane Matthew

To call it duende wouldn't be right.

This was a new death.
        Full of rage.
        Full of cold air.
        Full of salted breath and gusts of tears.

It curls around the Spanish roof tiles
        slowly flinging them off like a petty woman counting change.

It rakes against the faux stucco walls
        piercing howls tapping against the front door.

It builds with teach flicker of power, the hum electric of music and light quickly shutting down any hope of moving on.

The leaves, yes, only the leaves are spared.
        They wave and drip and sway and fight.

But still, the world is all green and water.

Power lines like tendrils along the Coin Laundry's façade.

Lito's eyes watch God.
He goes outside with his father.

First real hurricane—all is adventure until the trunks break, until I rush them back inside.

With a holler, Mateo shakes our home.
                      In Florida, the blues are really grey, a new duende.

Desarraigada

My daughter climbs into my bed
every morning
around 3 am.

She curls into my arm,
the one I keep outstretched for her
even in my sleep
as though I wait for her in my dreams.

She nestles her face into my neck.
I breathe in her curls
and soft skin.

I hold her as she turns over,
my hand touching her heart.

I used to tell myself I wasn't prepared to be a mother,
but really, I'm afraid to die.

Why does motherhood turn us into roots:
the kind our abuelas taught us to boil,
the kind our children consume.

Conjuro for the Lonely Daughter

I drink wine that has turned.

I listen to water that drips from
the upstairs neighbor's balcony.

The hum from the Heineken sign
we've only used once or twice
pulses as the breeze
rains its cool breath
on my face.
The night March air calms
the tear stains on my cheeks.

My father told me
he was getting married
four days ago,
and I only now
know what this means.
I picture my mother's grave,
a hallowed place
I haven't visited in 6 years.

Street lamps glow
against the Spanish tiles.
They look like the roof
of my father's house,
a place this other woman
now claims as her own.

The courtyard is silent,
cats long gone,
hunting their mice and birds
as I unravel
while dragging from Louie's pen.

The sky is a dusty cobalt
and I think of the March night
eight years ago,
just before we put

my mother
in the ground,
when all I wanted
was someone
to cry into.

Now Louie leaves me
as I sit,
this Florida magic
turning me
into the crone.

I drink and I smoke and yet I still feel too much.

My abuela has a recipe
for this, hidden
somewhere in her
arthritic knuckles.

If she were here,
she would boil a root
and sing an old song
I've never heard,
then tell me
to drink the tea,
but that I shouldn't
use honey this time.

What is magic but memory but song.

Florida Gothic #3: I-10 to Lake City

I notice the first piece as I drive home from school,
    rushing to pick up my kids before day care closes,
        rushing to lie down after a day of teaching 5th graders how to
            cite textual evidence from poetry.

The jagged edges of the watermelon are lined with dirt.
    Bits are strewn across the highway,
        the amaranth meat slowly turning the color of old ballet slippers.

After merging on to I-95 south,
    I see a broken shovel on the shoulder of the road,
        the blade splintered from the shaft.

I exit onto Beach Boulevard,
    The overpass above me lined with cars,
        A white man in a red hat knuckle deep in frustration as the cars
            trudge slowly across the sky.

I finally arrive to day care minutes before closing,
    My son's golden brown curls caked in a sweet juice,
    My infant daughter's eyes filled with fire and molasses.

Just smile more.

I am pouring out of my skin.
I am melting into my blankets.

My neck has been tense for 3 months.

I went to the gym this morning.
I drank 8 glasses of water today.
But I ate a chocolate chip pancake for
breakfast. I'm

becoming undone.

I open my computer to
create my lesson plan to
write a poem to
stalk my coworkers who won't be friends with me to
check my submissions to
surf Amazon for some good deals to
google symptoms of depression.

I've been in bed for 4 hours.
Baby girl cries and I stare.

I text Adeola "Do you ever feel
like you've crawled out of a ripped open sky?"

I had a dream last night.
    All my teeth fell out.
    I swallowed a water moccasin.
    Gold dripped from my eyes.
    My mother brushed her fingers through my hair
    as she sang a healing spell.
    I walked away from her and
    fell off a cliff
    and woke up.

A series of Facebook updates after Hurricane Irma.

1.

'Tis the 7th hour of the morn. Notos has released his lover Irma onto our beloved village. The children sleep, awaiting Hypnos' release. Our humble home still stands, electricity powering food storage and air conditioning. Leaks have sprung throughout our quaint condo, however, and I fear we may have unforeseeable damage on the horizon. Even so, all is well. We are dry, warm, and safe. Until next time dear ones.

With all my heart,
Michelle

P.S. Writing Facebook posts by candlelight truly changes your perspective on adjectives and cause and effect.

2.

The elders of the house have taken to the patio. Lady Violet rests in our bed chamber, napping after a restless night. Outside, Apollo seems to have lost his chariot again. Young Carlos examines the earth, taking sample of greenery, mud, and dirt. Lord Louie and I attempt contact with the outside world, wi-fi connection be damned. Irma's breath can still be felt in our midst, slamming doors and branches against our sturdy abodes. The rain has stopped though the still-standing water is ever present.

Until next time,
Michelle

3.

It seems Fortune has taken her golden skirts elsewhere. Our power is gone. Young Carlos struggles to overcome his desire for Peppa Pig. Lady Violet sits at her father's feet. Praise be that we prepared for this moment. We have taken to worshiping Dionysus, our hoppy elixirs and the gentle evening zephyrs luring us to an equilibrium only found post storm.

May our previous fortune find its way to you,
Michelle

4.
A southern stillness, thick as molasses, has filled
the air. The toads have regained their voices, croaking
into the twilight. When a Northerner asks me what it
means to experience a hurricane, I think of a picture of
four Cuban men sitting at a card table, bodies waste
deep in flood water, fichas clipping the quiet air.
Lager warms my belly as I make my way inside,
realizing I am one of the privileged ones, realizing
I know nothing of what it means to survive.

Naranja y Sal

After Chef Christina Martinez

pinch
rub
squeeze
pour
feel
smell
lick
crack
kiss

home.

The orange in my hand
the rind
       green and the color of Spanish roof tiles
the salt in my nose
       on my fingertips.

We rub this bird
we open new holes with a steak knife
stuff them with garlic y naranja y sal
and we layer on the bacon
and we try to remember our mother and what she taught us
and we try to remember our mother
and we try to remember the recipe
and we try not to cry
but we are naranja y sal
but we are bitter
and she is dead.

We honor the woman
the garlic
we honor the bird
we, the naranja y sal
we the bitter
give thanks
we honor

and we open new holes
with our words our loves our children our hands.

This trinity of naranja
        y sal
        y garlic.

This trinity of sorrow
           of motherhood
           of life.

15 Ways of Looking at a Latina

They call us Arcelia
    Treasure; altar of heaven
They call us Diosdada
    Determined; God given
They call us Olga
    Light; holy
They call us Ester
    Star; myrtle leaf
They call us Xiomara
    Battle ready; famous in war
They call us Carmen
    Song; garden
They call us Milagros
    Miracles; marvels
They call us muchacha
    Girl; maid
They call us guapa
    Beautiful; bold
They call us chonga
    Working class; Sexually and emotionally expressive
They call us mami
    Mother; sexy
They call us pendeja
    Vulgar; idiot
They call us peluda
    Swarthy; hairy
They call us puta
    Prostitute; slut
They call us Latina
    Only if we are the right shade of brown.

My [   ] was a racist.

1.
Second grade.
Book report.
Record yourself as the character in your book.

I said, "Ok."
I said, "Mami help."

The book was about a girl
        who was enslaved.
She'd learned how to read.
She taught others how to read.
I'd never read anything like that before.

Mami said, "We have to get some makeup."
Mami said, "Pick something dark brown."
Mami said, "Hold still. We can't let your skin show."

We played out the scene,
        Southern accent sounding foreign on our Miami tongues.

My sister chomped an apple
        while looking for the camera.

I turned the video in.
My teacher said nothing.
No one said anything.

2.
I'm in college.
It's Halloween.
I see my mother's kimono.
I pull it over my shoulders.
I pull my hair in a bun.
Everyone thinks I'm Asian, anyway,
I say to myself, to my friends.

3.
I'm in grad school.
My last month in NYC.
I buried my mother two months before.
I compile a thesis.
My roommates and I—
we throw a party.
Chongas vs. Guidos we said.
I slick my hair down
Paint my lips red
My eyes black.
I turn into the woman
I desperately
want to be.
Classmates ask *Why?* and *Are you sure?*
And we laugh and laugh and laugh.

4.
I want to ask her why she did that.
I want to ask her why we had to paint our skin.
I want to ask me why I had to wear a kimono.
I want to ask us why we had to pick that theme.
I want to ask her
  want to ask me
      to ask us
         ask her
            me
        ask

The fuck were you thinking.
      fuck were   thinking.
The   **were you**   .
The fuck   you thinking.
~~The fuck were you~~   .

WHAT THE FUCK WERE YOU THINKING.

She's dead though.

I look at Lito.

I look at Violet.
I look at Louie.
    at my students.
    at my classmates.
        my coworkers.
            friends.

What will they want to ask me when I'm dead though?

I'm not white but…

Aka, Who watches the watchmen?

I'm not white but,
I wear my whiteness on my face,
in my hair,
in my throat.

I move in spaces never meant for someone like me.
It's easy to do so when I look like my paler ancestors.

I think about my husband
and children—
how they will never know this freedom

      [read: *privilege*].

I watch the news
tick by.
Another Man
        Child
        Woman
        Person
was killed today.
They say they were aggressive

      [read: *deserved it*].

Will it be my husband next
on a drive through Brunswick
on the way to a school
that needs new cleaning supplies
for their kitchen?

Will it be my daughter in two decades
mouthing off to an officer
who pulled her out of traffic
when she was late for class
and speeding?

Will it be my son
running home from the corner store
his summer color—

    [read: *threat*]—

Frosty soda and gummy worms
hidden in his pocket
before he had a chance to slow down
his gait?

Do I think my whiteness will save them
if we get pulled over
on a drive down to Orlando
when it's late at night
and my taillight goes out?

Will my whiteness save them
or will it make me witness

[read: *accomplice*]

to murder?

Heirloom

I see my mother in my daughter's hair
curls begging to be unbridled
only craving the heat of the sun.

I remember my mother sitting on her bed,
crouched beneath a portable
hooded hair dryer
slight glances at the TV
so she could read the
subtitles.

I hear my mother tell me
that I have my father's
pelo lacio, and I'm lucky.

I stopped cutting my hair for a year and a half,
letting the ends grow frayed and split.

I tried to do my hair for a wedding
I sprayed and moussed and curled
and ringlets formed
but when I stepped outside
the humid air drowned them.

My daughter runs her fingers
through my hair
getting crumbs and juice in the strands
and I kiss her forearm and thank her
for this blessing
of knowing her.

My father's wife tells me
her hair will be beautiful
if her curls

grow

down

and I reply
her hair is already beautiful
because like Violet
it will do as it pleases.

I rub hair cream between my palms
an organic concoction of oils and butters.
I work the mixture into Violet's curls and watch
them shine and coil and live.

I think of my mother as I do my daughter's hair,
the stories she would tell me of my abuela
cursing her rizos
brushing her tendrils into submission.

I tell my daughter she is beautiful
with her dark curls and brown skin.

In this way, curses are broken.

When you turn 52.

You are now the age your mother never was.

You've never seen an empty nest before—
    space and clutter.

Who are you
    when no one
        depends on you?

Here are some instructions your mother couldn't leave behind:

    Step out to the yard
    barefoot. Dig your toes
    through the earth.
    Breathe her in.

    Pluck a mamey.
    Smell it.
    Hold it to the sun.
    Consume it.
    Plant the seed
    where your feet stand.

    Speak a poem
    you will never
    write down.
    Your conjuros
    will only be true
    in this way.

    Break off an aloe leaf.
    Extract the gel.
    Rub it on your palms
        your cheeks
        your thighs
        your chest.
    Say thank you.

    Lay down.

Watch the clouds drift.
Watch the sun fall.
Breathe in the Florida sunset.

Go back inside.
Boil ginger.
Pour it
in a copper mug.
Let it burn your tongue.

When your husband asks
      where you've been,
tell him

you've been alive.

Additional Acknowledgments

Invasive Species is a work 15 years in the making. What began as my graduate thesis, Mother City, has evolved into a reckoning, a collection of poems spanning maternal ancestry to my young daughter. Through it all, I have a few key people to thank.

First, I need to thank my husband, Louie Keller. Thank you for watching the kids while I toiled away on this manuscript, visited workshops across the country, and took afternoon writing sessions in our local coffee shops. Your dedication to my art and our family has finally paid off.

Secondly, I need to thank the Jacksonville literary community. In no particular order, thank you to Andres Rojas, who read early drafts of this manuscript and gave me essential feedback, Rashawd Hawkins who helped me edit and revise many of the poems present in this text, Jessica Q. Stark and Dorsey Craft who have helped build literary spaces in our weird wonderful city, Tiffany Melanson, who continuously speaks life and art into me, and the whole What's in a Verse crew for listening to me workshop these poems to death.

Lastly, I need to thank my mother, Lizet P. Flores. Because of you, this book exists. I almost didn't go to NYU when you got sick. Thank God I didn't listen to myself. Thank you for pushing me and believing in me enough so that I could become the working artist I am today. You never got to see your dreams fulfilled. Because of you, I will never give up on mine.

Born in Miami to Cuban-American parents, **Michelle Lizet Flores** is a proud Florida native. She graduated from Florida State University's undergraduate creative writing program. After graduating, she pursued her MFA in creative writing with a concentration in poetry from New York University. Unfortunately, Michelle's mother passed away just before her graduation, causing her to take a break from writing and pursue a career in K12 education. She was a 2011 Teach For America corps member, serving students in Memphis, Tennessee. After living in Memphis for 4 years, she moved to Jacksonville, Florida. Since moving to Jacksonville, she has published two chapbooks of poetry—*Cuentos from the Swamp* (a finalist for the Juan Felipe Herrera Award for poetry) and *Memoria*. Her previously published poems can be found in *The Miami Rail, Chircú Journal*, and *Travel Latina*. Her short fiction has been published through Flowersong Press. She has also published a children's picture book—*Carlito the Bat Learns to Trick or Treat*. After a short stint in San Antonio, Texas, she returned to Jacksonville to co-host the What's in a Verse open mic in the historic Five Points neighborhood. Aside from co-hosting and open mic and writing, she is a creative writing teacher at Douglas Anderson School for the Arts. *Invasive Species* is her first published full-length collection of poems. She can be reached on most social media platforms as @shellyflowers. You can also find her at her website: michellelizetflores.com.

www.ingramcontent.com/pod-product-compliance
Lightning Source LLC
Chambersburg PA
CBHW020340170426
43200CB00006B/442